Saving It For Albie

A play

Richard Harris

Samuel French — London
www.samuelfrench-london.co.uk

Copyright © 2012 by Wishbone Ltd
All Rights Reserved

SAVING IT FOR ALBIE is fully protected under the copyright laws of the British Commonwealth, including Canada, the United States of America, and all other countries of the Copyright Union. All rights, including professional and amateur stage productions, recitation, lecturing, public reading, motion picture, radio broadcasting, television and the rights of translation into foreign languages are strictly reserved.

ISBN 978-0-573-11388-8

www.samuelfrench.co.uk
www.samuelfrench.com

FOR AMATEUR PRODUCTION ENQUIRIES

UNITED KINGDOM AND WORLD EXCLUDING NORTH AMERICA
plays@samuelfrench.co.uk
020 7255 4302/01

Each title is subject to availability from Samuel French, depending upon country of performance.

CAUTION: Professional and amateur producers are hereby warned that *SAVING IT FOR ALBIE* is subject to a licensing fee. Publication of this play does not imply availability for performance. Both amateurs and professionals considering a production are strongly advised to apply to the appropriate agent before starting rehearsals, advertising, or booking a theatre. A licensing fee must be paid whether the title is presented for charity or gain and whether or not admission is charged.

The Professional Rights in this play are controlled by The Agency Ltd, 24 Pottery Lane, Holland Park, London W11 4LZ.

No one shall make any changes in this title for the purpose of production. No part of this book may be reproduced, stored in a retrieval system, or transmitted in any form, by any means, now known or yet to be invented, including mechanical, electronic, photocopying, recording, videotaping, or otherwise, without the prior written permission of the publisher. No one shall upload this title, or part of this title, to any social media websites.

The right of Richard Harris to be identified as author of this work has been asserted in accordance with Section 77 of the Copyright, Designs and Patents Act 1988.

SAVING IT FOR ALBIE

First produced as a platform production at the Tabard Theatre, London, on 25th May 2012.

Rose Patricia Brake
Grace Anita Graham
Ray Ian Ashpitel
Albie Paul Thornley

Directed by Guy Retallack

CHARACTERS

Rose, 60s
Grace, her daughter, mid-40s
Ray, late 40s
Albie, Ray's brother, younger by two years

SYNOPSIS OF SCENES

The action of the play takes place in a second floor flat in a modern block near the canal in Manchester.

ACT I Early summer, afternoon
ACT II A moment or so later

Time — the present

For Miss G

Other plays by Richard Harris
published by Samuel French Ltd

Albert
The Business of Murder
Dead Guilty
Death In High Heels (adapted from the book by Christianna Brand)
A Foot in the Door
Ghosts (adapted from Henrik Ibsen)
Going Straight
In Two Minds
Is It Something I Said?
Keeping Mum (from Visiting Hour)
Large as Life
(music and additional lyrics by Keith Strachan)
Local Affairs
The Maintenance Man
Outside Edge
Party Piece
Stepping Out
Stepping Out the Musical
(lyrics by Mary Stewart-David and music by Denis King)
Two and Two Make Sex (with Leslie Darbon)
Visiting Hour

ACT I

A second floor flat in a modern block near the canal in Manchester. Early summer afternoon

Lightly curtained french windows lead out on to a terrace. There is an open plan kitchen separated from the main area by a breakfast bar, two doors — each to an ensuite bedroom, an archway giving on to a small lobby, a cupboard and the main door. It's very much the bachelor pad. The only signs of anything out of place are a woman's coat and small handbag on a chair, an empty glass tumbler, and a large hat on the sofa. And, sitting next to the hat, is Rose

Rose is in her 60s. She is dressed in a tasteful frock that matches the discarded coat. A thin woman, not unattractive in her day. She sits upright on the sofa, pen in hand, book of crossword puzzles on her lap. After a moment, she thinks she has worked out a clue, taps her pen against the book to check the letters, realizes the word doesn't fit and clicks her tongue irritably. After a moment, she decides she's had enough of the puzzle and sets book and pen to one side. She returns to sitting upright, examining her surroundings with mild disapproval. Disapproval is her default mode. Having taken in her surroundings — not for the first time — she remains sitting, slowly tapping one hand against the other, as though counting off the seconds she is waiting. She is not a woman who sits still. She glances down at the hat, frowns, and takes it up to adjust the applied silk flower on the crown. She replaces the hat. Again, the sense of impatience, of needing something to do. So she takes up the empty tumbler and is moving to the kitchen when the telephone rings

Rose (*flatly*) Not again.

She pours water into the tumbler as the phone cuts out after four rings and the answerphone kicks in

Albie's Voice This is Albert. Don't ask where I am, you'll only get jealous, just leave me a message or try the mobile which no doubt you already have.
Rose You certainly fancy yourself, don't you, Mister?

Woman's Voice It's me and yes I have tried the mobile *and* left a message. So I'll say it again — is it true, you silly bugger? I don't believe it. Anyway, you know where I am if you want to show me the photographs — ta-ta.

The phone clicks off. Again Rose gives a disparaging little jerk of the head as she stands, sipping water. Then, hearing a key in the door, she moves quickly to sit on the sofa, taking up a handkerchief so that she is weakly mopping her brow

Grace comes in, leaving the door partly open. She is in her mid 40s. Blonde and attractive, she is taller than average and somewhat lacking in co-ordination. She is wearing a pretty frock and high heels. She is carrying a small bridal bouquet and three or four gift-wrapped presents

Grace (*immediately*) How are you feeling?
Rose I've still got my head, thank you.
Grace Oh dear.

Grace puts down the presents near the archway and attempts to feel her mother's head but she is waved away

Rose Stop fussing.
Grace Did you take your pills?
Rose Oh for goodness' sake.
Grace (*indicating*) You managed to do your crossword then.
Rose I glanced at it to take my mind off things, yes.

It's clearly a typical and perfunctory exchange. Grace goes into the kitchen and puts the little bouquet in water

Grace It all went very well I thought.

No response

Didn't *you*?
Rose (*flatly*) Very nice. (*She reaches for her handbag and puts the book and pen into it*) I didn't think you'd be back this early.
Grace Oh, it was just a drink — you know — everyone had to get back to work — well, what d'you think?
Rose Think?
Grace The flat.

Rose It's not exactly what you'd call homely, is it?
Grace It will be.
Rose I thought you'd prefer to start married life in a place of your own.
Grace Have you seen the terrace?
Rose Oh, that's what it is — where's your husband?
Grace They're on their way up.
Rose They? Who's they?
Grace Albie — and Raymond.
Rose Raymond?
Grace He's giving Albie a hand — (*and for the first time she shows some concern*) — Mum — don't say anything — please.
Rose About what?
Grace Just don't say anything — please.

There's a polite tap at the door

Ray (*calling, off*) Gracie!
Grace (*calling back*) Come through, Raymond.
Rose (*under her breath*) It's Grace Andrews, not Gracie bloody Fields.

But her face changes as

> *Ray and Albie enter. Ray has Albie over his shoulder in a fireman's carry. They are brothers, solidly built, both in their late 40s, Ray the elder by a couple of years. They are in suits, Albie's much sharper but crumpled. Both men have bedraggled buttonholes. Albie is drunkenly, fitfully, giving his version of "Singing In The Rain"*

Grace moves across to help but doesn't know how

Grace It would be today the lift isn't working.
Ray Sod's law, int' it? (*He hands her a key*)
Grace I don't know how you managed.
Ray I'm used to it — where would you like him?

Albie ups the volume of his "Singing In The Rain" for half a line before going back to a mumble. Rose watches it all in not unhappy disbelief

Grace I think perhaps he should go on the bed, what d'you think?
Ray Right. Hello again, Mrs Andrews.

Rose manages a sort of smile and vague raising of the hand

Ray Come on, Sunshine, time to sleep it off.

He turns towards the bedroom but Albie starts jerking about

Albie Put me down, you bugger ... put me down I tell you.

His arms and legs are flailing and Ray looks to Grace, indicating that he'd better do as he's told, and lowers Albie carefully to the floor. Albie tries to point a warning finger at Ray

   Next time ... next time ... bloody ask. Where's my wife?
Grace Here I am, darling.

He focuses on her and gives her a beaming smile

Albie This is my wife.
Ray I know.
Albie You look lovely, bloody lovely. Doesn't she?
Ray She does.
Albie You do. Bloody lovely.

He stands there, wavering. Grace moves to him and takes his hand and rubs it gently

Grace Listen, sweetheart ... why don't you have a little lie-down for a bit?
Albie Because ... I don't want a little lie-down for a bit.
Ray Come on, Albie. (*He attempts to take Albie's arm*)
Albie (*snapping*) Bugger off.

He stands wavering for a moment then, attempting dignity, moves to the sofa, stands wavering in front of it as if about to make some important pronouncement ... but gives up and is about to plonk himself down — on Rose's hat — when Grace, realizing, snatches it away from under him. She puts it on a side table. Albie sits and turns bleary eyes on Rose sitting next to him

   I know you. (*He gives a big broad smile but the smile fades and his eyes close and he slumps back into the sofa, legs sprawled*)

A moment, and:

Grace What d'you think?

Ray I think best leave him. For the time being anyway.
Rose Far be it from me, but I would have thought a cup of black coffee was called for.
Grace Good idea. (*She's on her way to the kitchen*) How about you, Raymond?
Ray (*looking at his watch*) I think perhaps I should —
Grace At least have a cup of coffee or something, all the running about you've done.
Ray Yes, but you won't want me —
Grace Please.

The "please", unstressed though it was, doesn't go unnoticed

Ray Lovely. Thanks.

He smiles. She returns the smile and busies in the kitchen

   Could you make it tea?
Grace Course I could. You'll have a cup, will you, Mum?
Rose If it's not too much trouble. (*She gives Ray her regal smile*) When in doubt, reach for the teapot.

Ray gives her a little smile back. This moment

Ray You feeling better now, are you, Mrs Andrews?
Rose Much better, thank you, Raymond.

A little moment

Ray You had quite a nasty turn.
Rose I get these terrible migraines.

Albie shifts and scratches his crotch

   Brought on by stress.

The following will be punctuated by Albie's shifting and verbal noises

   I must say you've been very supportive, Raymond.
Grace Yes, you have.
Rose I'm sure Grace is very appreciative.
Grace I am.
Ray Yeah — well — best man and all that.

Rose (*making light, but with an edge*) I would have thought making sure the bridegroom has got the ring is one thing but carrying him up two flights of stairs surely comes under the heading of above and beyond.
Ray Well, weddings, these things happen, don't they?
Rose Yes, I suppose you're right. Although quite why, I've never really understood. (*To Grace*) I mean, look at your cousin Leslie's wedding. Arriving at the church in that state, tie under his ear, oil all over his new suit.
Grace (*to Ray*) The exhaust fell off the car.
Rose And him supposed to be a mechanic.
Grace A dental mechanic, Mum — he makes false teeth.
Rose And what he said to that poor vicar. *And* his new wife having to stand there and listen. No wonder the marriage didn't last. But at least they had a proper church wedding.

Grace brings over two mugs of tea

Grace There we are, Mum, sorry about the mug — d'you take sugar, Ray?
Ray No, no, that's fine.
Grace We didn't *want* a church wedding: either of us.
Rose I'm just *saying*. (*She mouths to Ray*) She can be so touchy.

They sip their tea as Albie gets through a line or two of "Singing In The Rain" and Grace takes a mug of coffee to him

Grace Here we are, love ... drink some of this.

She gently attempts to rouse him. He opens one eye and then both and tries to focus on her

Albie What's happening?
Grace You've had a little too much to drink.

He takes this information in

Albie I have, yes.

He thinks about it, then scrabbles in his jacket pocket and pulls out a packet of cigarettes, gets one into his mouth, scrabbles into a trouser pocket and pulls out an iPhone, holds it to the cigarette as though to light it, realizes

Act I

(*Blearily, to no one in particular*) Iss those antibiotics I've been on. (*He shoves it back into his pocket and pulls out a lighter. He is about to light up but remembers, takes the cigarette from his mouth. Very seriously*) No smoking in the flat. That's ... one of the ... new ... rules. (*He studiously returns the cigarette to the packet and puts the packet and lighter on a side table, patting them into place*)

Grace Why don't you have a little lie-down?

Again, he takes in the idea

Albie I'm going to have a little lie-down.

He attempts to get to his feet. Rose cowers away from him. Ray moves quickly to assist him

Are you still here?
Ray I'm still here and you're still pissed — (*to Rose*) — I beg your pardon.
Rose None taken.

Albie, hearing her voice, beams at her

Albie Hello, Mother-in-law. (*Which reminds him*) Where's my wife?
Grace I'm here, darling.
Albie That's my wife, that is.
Ray So you keep telling us.
Albie We just got married. Didn't we, my lovely woman?
Grace We did, yes, and you've done a bit too much celebrating.
Albie (*slowly wagging a finger at her*) I've been very very naughty.
Ray Come on, let's get you on that bed.

He half-carries, half-supports Albie towards one of the bedrooms

Albie I have. Very, very naughty.

They go into the bedroom, Albie still wagging his finger

Rose Pass me my pills, will you? They're in my bag.

Grace fetches the handbag

Why you have to wear such high heels, I've no idea.

Grace He likes me in high heels. (*Smiling to herself*) He says he likes me looking down at him. (*Gently*) Mum ... it's for me to worry about, not you. And I'm not worried about it, I'm really not, because I know it's not like him. It's just — nerves, that's all.
Rose Oh well. That's all right then.
Grace You'll really like him. I promise you.

Ray comes out of the bedroom, quietly closing the door

Albie can be heard vaguely calling out for his wife

Ray He says he wants to see you, but maybe — you know.
Grace No — I'll go — I've got his coffee, anyway. Thanks, Ray.

She takes the mug of coffee into the bedroom, closing the door

Rose Come and sit down and finish your tea. (*She smiles up at him*)

He returns the smile as best he can and resumes sitting, taking up his mug to sip the tea

    Can I ask you something, Raymond?
Ray What's that?
Rose I'm not asking you to betray a confidence.
Ray (*smiling*) If it is, I won't.
Rose I mean I know he's your brother and everything but I really do have to ask.
Ray Ask away then.
Rose Is he — you know.
Ray Is he what?
Rose Does he — you know. (*She makes a small mime of "drink"*)
Ray You mean —— ? (*He makes a bigger mime of it*)
Rose Yes.
Ray No. He likes his pint, but no more than the rest of us. No.
Rose Only when you said — you're used to it.
Ray (*not with it*) Did I?
Rose When you — brought him in.

Ray works it out and grins

Ray I meant carrying. I did two years in the fire service.
Rose Oh I see. And there was me thinking ——
Ray No, you've nothing to worry about on that score.

Act I

Rose But you do understand — as Grace's mother — and not really knowing him.
Ray Course I do.
Rose I mean, when she suddenly comes round and tells me she's getting married to someone I've never even met.
Ray I can imagine.
Rose I mean, no warning, nothing.
Ray Aye.
Rose I mean, Grace of all people.
Ray She's a lovely girl, Mrs Andrews — and he's a lucky fellah.
Rose Oh, don't misunderstand me — what I'm saying is ... well ... perhaps another time ... (*She smiles as though suppressing a wealth of sadness ... and "realizes" she is holding her bottle of pills*)
Rose You won't mind if I take my pills, will you?
Ray No, no — you — you know — go ahead.
Rose I do try to manage without but ... migraine really is a curse, you know.
Ray Our mother used to get migraines.
Rose I've had it all my adult life.
Ray Hers used to come on —
Rose Well, after Grace was born.
Ray — right out of the —
Rose Sometimes there's nothing for it but to lie in a darkened room. People all too often don't really understand just how debilitating it is.

A moment. Ray is aware of how little Rose is interested in someone else's problems

Ray No. (*He smiles*)

She bravely manages to force down a pill with her tea, sighs, and returns the pills to her handbag

Rose You know, Raymond ... I don't think I thanked you properly for driving me here.

Ray is happy to change the subject

Ray No trouble. It's what I do. You know — driver.
Rose With the fire brigade.
Ray No no, that was years ago.
Rose So you mean like mini-cabs?
Ray No, no, top of the range stuff.

Rose (*pronouncing it "en Français"*) A chauffeur, you mean.
Ray (*grinning*) I suppose I am, aye.
Rose I thought your car was rather smart.
Ray Has to be. We do — you know — an executive service.
Rose Oh. Executive.
Ray Mostly. You know.
Rose You don't wear a uniform though.
Ray You mean a cap and stuff.
Rose Well I suppose —
Ray No, no, nothing like that. Just a suit. (*Slight pause*) This suit, as a matter of fact.

She nods her understanding, happy that he doesn't wear a cap and stuff. A pause

Rose When you say "we" —
Ray It's not my business. I'm just — you know.
Rose One day no doubt.
Ray (*grinning*) We'll see, eh? Anyway, I'm glad you're feeling better — not much fun coming all this way and then — you know.
Rose I felt so terrible, causing all that fuss.
Ray You can't help being poorly.
Rose I don't think Grace was very happy.
Ray No, she was fine.
Rose I don't think so.
Ray I'm sure she was.
Rose No, I don't think so.

This moment

Ray Day my niece — Rene — got married, we all went round to the house — before she and Colin — that's her husband — got there — and put putty in all the keyholes.
Rose Oh yes? (*She'd rather be re-living her past than listening to someone else's*)
Ray They had to break a window to get in. Colin cut his hand to the bone, Rene had hysterics — although I suspect more than anything because of the blood on the new carpet — and they spent their first night in Accident and Emergency.

Grace comes out of the bedroom, quietly closing the door. She is holding Albie's buttonhole

During the next she takes it into the kitchen and puts it in water

Act I

Grace Sleeping like a baby, can you believe.
Ray Give him half an hour, he'll be right as rain and begging for forgiveness.
Grace (*laughing*) Albie? Begging? I don't think so.

The phone rings. Grace is undecided about answering it and the answer machine cuts in

Albie's Voice This is Albert. Don't ask where I am, you'll only get jealous, just —

Grace switches off the machine and moves away

Rose Aren't you going to see who it is?
Grace They'll call back if it's important. (*She rubs the back of one hand with the palm of the other, something she does when she is mentally off-balance or biting her tongue*)
Rose I think you should answer it, Grace, it could be an emergency.
Grace We don't do emergencies.
Rose I don't understand her, I really don't.
Grace Then don't try, it will bring on one of your headaches.

So often Grace suppresses defensive responses to her mother, but every now and again, she can't resist a little fight back

Rose Sarcasm doesn't become you, Grace.
Grace You're right, I'm sorry. Right then, Mum, time you were making a move — quarter past five your train.
Ray I'll take you to the station.
Rose You most certainly will not, you've done enough running around for one day.
Grace I'll get you a taxi.
Ray No, you won't — I'm taking you and it will be a pleasure.
Grace Ray.
Ray Don't argue, Mrs Rodway — I said — it'll be a pleasure.
Rose You're very kind, Raymond.

He pulls out his mobile phone and indicates it

Ray I'll just phone Debbie — let her know what's happening — all right?
Grace Of course it's all right.

He goes out on to the terrace, already dialling, sliding the windows closed after him. He can be seen, pacing, using the phone throughout

Grace We shouldn't take advantage of him.
Rose He offered.
Grace Because he's like that. (*She gives a little wave to Ray*)
Rose Have you seen how many messages there are?
Grace What?
Rose The *telephone*.
Grace Oh for God's sake.
Rose It never stops ringing.
Grace (*"patiently"*) It's our wedding day. There are bound to be people calling. For all sorts of reasons.
Rose Who's Ingrid?
Grace Ingrid?
Rose Three times she's phoned.
Grace I've no idea. (*Which isn't true*)
Rose Well that's not very nice, is it?
Grace (*over-patiently*) What isn't?
Rose People phoning and you don't know who they are.
Grace Oh this is silly.

Ray comes in from the terrace

Ray No problem.
Grace Are you sure?
Ray She's going over to see our daughter anyway.
Grace Not because —
Ray No no no — it was all arranged. I'd forgotten. (*He smiles at Rose*) Anyway: whenever you're ready, Mrs A.
Rose Actually ... I've been thinking. Perhaps it would be better for me to catch a later train.
Grace Why?
Rose Well, in case you need some help.
Grace Why would I need help?
Rose Oh Grace, come now.
Ray Excuse me, but if you mean Albie —
Rose Well he's not exactly in the best of conditions, is he?
Grace He's had a bit too much to drink, that's all.
Rose And we all know where that can lead, don't we?
Ray Honestly, Mrs —
Rose What time's the next train?
Grace Mum.

Act I   13

Rose What time is the next train?

Unseen by Rose, Grace gives Ray a helpless little gesture

Ray There's one every half hour or so.
Rose Well then.
Grace Mum —
Rose I'm your mother. I just want to make sure you're all right. Unless you want to send me away worrying.

This moment

Grace No of course I don't. I wasn't thinking. (*She gives a flat smile*) Catch the next one. (*"Brightly"*) Does anyone want another tea?
Ray No, you're all right, thanks.
Rose What I *would* like is the use of your toilet — I know where it is, thank you. (*To Ray*) Excuse me.

She goes into the second bedroom. A moment

Grace Sorry.
Ray What for?
Grace The way she — takes over.
Ray You know — mothers.
Grace I know *my* mother.

They smile

What was the name of the chap taking photographs?
Ray Billy.
Grace That's right, Billy. He said he works with Albert.
Ray He does, yes. But he really wants to be a photographer.
Grace I hope they come out all right.
Ray He's good, Billy, he won't let you down. Course, it's all on computer nowadays.
Grace Just as well — he can airbrush me into a decent shape.
Ray You look really lovely.
Grace I wish.
Ray You do.
Grace Oh Raymond ... I'm long and I'm skinny and I've got little eyes and bad posture — I don't know what he sees in me, I really don't.

She has said it not with self-pity but with humour and as a matter of fact

Ray I tell you what else you've got. The same opinion of yourself and it's as daft now as it was then.
Grace You're very nice.
Ray I mean it.
Grace Thank you.

A moment

Ray It really is good to see you.
Grace You too.
Ray When he told me he'd met you again I couldn't believe it.
Grace I know.
Ray Bloody hell. I mean, what are the chances?
Grace I still can't believe he recognized me.
Ray Oh, you haven't changed that much.
Grace It's over twenty years, Ray.
Ray You really haven't.
Grace I didn't recognize *him* — not at first.
Ray Well he's about four stone heavier for a start. We both are.
Grace I mean, as soon as I looked at him properly ... I mean when I — you know — realized.
Ray Anyway. It's lovely. For the both of you.
Grace I don't know about him, but I feel — so lucky.
Ray And so does he.
Grace Yes, I think he does. Anyway, I hope so, I really hope so. (*But*) We'd better change the subject or I'll start blubbing.
Ray Right. What d'you think of United's chances next season?
Grace I don't know about that but I think I might be spending a lot of Saturday afternoons on my own.
Ray Well, I can make use of his ticket if you really put your foot down.
Grace Can you see that happening?
Ray Not really, no.

They smile

Gonna be a big change for you, moving up here.
Grace We'll manage.
Ray Course you will.

Rose returns

Rose Is everything all right?

Grace gives a little smile at Ray: as if it wouldn't be

Ray I was just saying it's going to be a big change for Grace, moving up here.
Rose Yes I know.
Grace It's only Manchester, not the Middle East.
Rose Yes, but you're not the most adventurous soul in the world, are you, darling? I mean, be fair.
Grace No, I'm not, no.
Rose No. (*Having won her point*) So it's just you and Albert, is it, Raymond?
Ray Sorry?
Rose In the family.
Ray Oh. Aye. Just us two.

She waits for more information

I'm the eldest. Two years.
Rose That's why you look after him, is it?
Ray I suppose it is, aye.
Rose Yes, it's usually the way, isn't it? Or should be. (*Apparently a dig at Grace*) And you've got three children.
Ray Two girls and a boy. Well, I say children, the eldest is twenty-three now.
Rose They're always children though, aren't they?
Ray Grandad, too.
Rose How lovely.
Ray Little Alice. She's nearly three. And Charlie. Eighteen months.
Rose Lovely.
Ray They are.

The telephone rings. After a few rings, Grace takes it up

Grace Hello? No, he isn't. Yes I am. Thank you. I will, yes. (*She replaces the receiver and jots down a name on the adjacent pad. On second thoughts she pulls the wire from the back of the phone*)
Rose All right? (*Meaning "who was it"?*)
Grace Fine. (*She makes it clear that no more information will be forthcoming*)
Rose Aren't you going to open your presents?

Grace has forgotten them

Grace We'll do it later. Together.

This moment

Rose Nice of people to bring presents.
Grace Yes.
Rose Those that did.
Ray You did say.
Grace We did — no presents.
Rose Still.

And she gets back to where she wants to be

(*To Ray*) Have you seen how many telephone messages there are, Raymond?
Grace And we'll *listen* to them. Later.
Rose (*"light"*) Later, everything's later. (*To Ray*) It's hardly stopped ringing.
Ray He does a lot of his business from here — that's the thing nowadays, intit?
Rose So my son tells me.
Ray An iPhone and a coupla credit cards and you're off and running.
Rose Who's Ingrid?
Ray Er ...
Rose Three times she's phoned, whoever she is.
Ray Oh — Ingrid — she's just — you know — a friend.
Rose Oh I see.
Ray You know — one of the crowd.
Rose She seems to find it very amusing — Albert getting married.
Ray Bound to be calls like that though, aren't there? First night of our honeymoon, phone never stopped ringing. It's sort of like traditional, people pulling your leg.
Rose For young people, Raymond, admittedly. But not for someone of Grace's age, surely?
Grace Have you heard from Martin lately?
Rose Oh yes, he phones every week. (*To Ray*) My son.
Ray Ah.
Grace I thought he might have been here.
Rose Oh Grace, you know how busy he is.
Grace Or at least phoned me or something.
Rose I'm sure he tried.
Grace I shouldn't think so. You did tell him, did you?
Rose You really do resent him, don't you? Sorry about this, Raymond.
Grace I don't resent him in the slightest.
Rose Oh you do, Grace, you know you do.
Grace I don't know him well enough.
Rose For goodness' sake, he's your *brother*.
Grace We've got the same parents, that's all.

Act I 17

Rose What a ridiculous thing to say.
Grace Is it?
Rose If your poor dear father was alive to hear you talking like this.
Grace But he's not, is he, Mum?

This moment

Ray My speech all right, was it?
Grace Lovely.
Ray I was petrified.
Rose And you a fireman.
Grace Petrified or not, it was just right. Thank you.
Ray He said it's not going to be a big do, but I'll want you to say a few words — you know, the usual — course, straight away me mind went blank and I said to him, come on Alb, give us a clue, you're good at stuff like this. Just keep it short, he says — with plenty of good jokes. Bloody hell. Anyway, he says, there's this site on the internet, so I — you know.
Grace (*smiling*) You done good.
Rose "Done good"?
Grace Football. "The boy done good."
Rose I've no idea what you're talking about.
Ray It's what managers say. When they're interviewed. On the telly.
Grace (*teasing*) Mum only watches *Panorama* — don't you, Mum?

Rose chooses not to answer, gives a little sniff. Grace gives a little smile at Ray. She's more concerned about Albie than she wants to let on. Silence. Which Ray breaks with

Ray Did you like the one about Popeye and Olive Oyl? Debbie thought it might not be suitable. Not that she really understood it. But then I don't think women laugh at jokes very much. They don't seem to find them necessary. Jokes. Fellahs? Take away jokes and they'd just be standing there looking at each other.

This moment

Rose My son was married in Mauritius. On a beach. With their feet in the sea. It was lovely, wasn't it, Grace?
Grace It was.
Rose I made a lovely dress for the bride. As a wedding present. In very pale silk chiffon. It hung beautifully. I was a seamstress, you know. (*Of her own dress*) I made this. And the coat. I would have made something for Grace of course, but not having any notice ...

Ray She looked lovely anyway. You both do.
Rose You old sprucer.
Ray Sprucer? Don't know that one.
Grace One of my dad's expressions. It means — what — flatterer. Don't think I've ever heard anyone else use it. He had quite a few funny old words like that, didn't he, Dad?
Rose The lady behind the bar — the elderly one with the short grey hair ...
Ray Hilda.
Rose I asked her for a glass of water and she said are you all right, love, you look starved and I didn't know for the life of me what she meant until someone said she means you look a bit cold.
Ray Oh aye — starved — yeah.
Rose We all have these different expressions, I suppose. Although in a few years I imagine we'll all be speaking the same. "Have a nice day". Where did *that* come from, I ask you.
Grace Same place it all comes from.
Ray Aye, true enough.
Rose That's what it will be, won't it? Praying to Allah in an American accent.
Grace You do like your *Daily Mail*, don't you, Mum?
Rose Yesterday, just as I was sitting down to my evening meal, the phone rang. I knew it would be one of them — you do, don't you, always at a meal time. Anyway, I answered it because you never know, do you, which of course they rely on, and this voice says am I speaking to Mrs Andrews and I said you are and he said hi there, Mrs Andrews, my name is Alan, how you doing? I said, let me tell you something, young man —
Grace I hope you weren't rude to him.
Rose — for a start, I said, I suspect rather than Alan your name is something like Achmed ... secondly, I have no doubt that you're phoning from somewhere on the sub-continent ... thirdly, no one in this country says "Hi there, how you doing" ... and lastly, whatever you're trying to sell me, I don't want it.
Grace He was only doing his job.
Rose Yes, well, I've never had your understanding about these things.
Grace I just think you've got to ... put yourself in their position.
Rose I am not criticizing the individual, he's got a right to earn a crust like everyone else, I am criticizing the way the world operates nowadays. And I'm quite sure that nine out of ten people agree with me. I don't know what it's like in Manchester, Raymond, but in London it's quite ridiculous. I mean, be honest, Grace — how many people working in your hotel were born in this country?

Act I

Grace Mum, we'll never see eye to eye on this so can we just drop it?
Rose Turn your nose up at me as much as you like, but twenty years time, we'll see. Well, *you'll* see, I won't be here.

This moment

It's funny, isn't it, Raymond? When you think, none of this would be happening if I hadn't dislocated my ankle.
Ray None of what — sorry?
Rose Did she not say? Did you not say?
Grace I don't think I did, no.
Rose But then that's what life's so often all about, isn't it? Of course, you can plan *some* things, a lot of things I suppose, some people, but very often it's pure chance — you get off the bus at the wrong stop or you arrive somewhere ten minutes early and your whole life takes a completely different turning — even if, as in your case, Grace, love, the turning was a lot further down the road — and even then, what were the chances of Albert meeting you again the way he did?
Grace Or even *me* meeting *him*.
Rose You know what I mean.
Grace (*making it light*) I know exactly what you mean.
Rose You have to be so careful with this girl. (*To Grace*) Would you rather I sat here saying nothing?
Grace Tell Raymond about your ankle.
Rose Not if you'd rather I didn't.
Grace Go on, Mum, you know you're dying to. Go on.

Rose considers and then

Rose We were going on holiday together, Raymond — my first time away since my husband died — oh, you tell him, Grace.
Grace It's your story.
Rose Yes, well, I've gone off it.
Grace (*still making it light*) D'you want to hear this, Ray?
Rose Of course he does, don't you, Raymond?
Ray Well, not unless you — you know.
Rose We were going on holiday together — off you go, Grace.

The last thing Grace wants to do is tell the story, but, once again, she decides on the easier route

Grace Actually, it was all very last minute — we didn't so much choose a place as get given a choice of two. Corfu or Malta I think it was.

Rose We're not paupers but we did have a budget to work to.
Grace So I booked the package — Corfu — came home and started packing — and Mum tripped over and put her ankle out.
Rose We're talking serious dislocation here — I was on a stick for over three weeks.
Grace I tried to cancel — I mean the whole idea was the both of us going.
Rose And be honest, sweetheart, it wasn't so much me not going as you not wanting to go on your own — she's never been very good at being on her own — nothing to be ashamed of, some people are, some people aren't.
Grace I actually quite enjoy being on my own. In the right circumstances.
Rose I'm not saying you don't, Grace, what I'm saying is that when it comes to this sort of situation — going on holiday — you're not really one to join in, are you? You're not much of a mixer. You must have seen that, Raymond, when you first met her.
Grace Mum, it was over twenty years ago.
Rose Well *you* remember.
Grace Yes, but Ray doesn't have to.
Ray I do, though, as it happens.
Rose After all those years.
Ray I mean, it all came back to me. Well, a lot of it. When Albie told me he'd met you again. (*He smiles, fondly remembering*) I can remember the first time we spoke.
Grace On the bus.
Ray Aye — on the bus. We were getting dropped off at the various hotels and we were the last ones — Albie and me and you and another couple.
Grace (*smiling*) Yes.
Ray You were *shy* I remember, but then you were on your own. Mind you, it's difficult to be on your own once Albie makes up his mind you shouldn't be.
Grace You were both very nice to me.
Rose Did you not wonder? A young woman on her own?
Ray Wonder what?
Rose *Why* she was on her own.
Ray Must have done, I suppose.
Grace What are you saying, Mum?
Rose I'm simply ——
Grace Why is it that people on their own are so often seen as objects of pity?
Rose Well it's not *usual*, is it?
Grace That's what I mean.

Act I

Rose Honestly, you talk in circles — she's always been the same, you know.
Grace "Lives in a world of her own."

Rose sighs patiently

Rose What I'm saying is ... you didn't say *why* you were on your own?
Grace I didn't say *you* specifically ... at least I shouldn't imagine I did ... I probably just said ... someone.
Rose Oh *I* see. You didn't want a couple of young lads to think you were the sort to go on holiday with your mother.
Grace Possibly. Probably.
Rose Well it's understandable. Not everyone's like you, are they, sweetheart?

A moment

Grace Anyway. As you say. None of this would have happened. I'll, umm, I'll just go and see how he is.

She goes into the bedroom

Rose (*after a moment*) *You* knew what I meant, didn't you, Raymond?
Ray About Grace being on her own? Not really.
Rose Oh I think so. I mean it's not as if it's an insult, is it? It's a fact. People on their own, you make assumptions.
Ray Doesn't mean you're right though, does it?
Rose No of course it doesn't. That's what I'm saying. One *assumes*.
Ray Not wishing to be rude, I mean you could say it's — you know — condescending.
Rose I would have thought human nature —
Ray All of us, I mean. I mean, I'm the same. When *I'm* on my own, I feel a right Mary Ann.
Rose (*flirty*) When are *you* ever on your own?
Ray Sometimes I have a job, maybe up to London or somewhere, and I have to hang around and I take myself off for a meal or something ... and I'd be a liar if I didn't say I feel awkward. So I try to bury me nose in a book or a newspaper and enjoy a nice quiet read but nine times out of ten I can't get out of there quick enough.
Rose I know what you mean. Yes. I do. Sadly, I do. (*She luxuriates in her sadness*)

Ray breaks the silence with a sudden thought

Ray Funny thing is though, it's not like that in a pub. A bloke can sit on his own having a quiet pint for as long as he likes and nobody looks at you twice. Funny that, int'it? Mind you, six o'clock at night, pubs are full of blokes sitting on their own having a pint. Not wanting to go home, I suppose. There you are, you see. Drawing conclusions. A woman on her own in a pub, now that's a different story.
Rose I can remember the time when a woman on her own wasn't *allowed* in a public house.
Ray (*grinning*) You don't want to go into the town centre of a Friday night then. Some of the sights *I've* seen.
Rose These young women, you mean.
Ray Frightens the life out of you.
Rose Oh I know: some of these documentaries you see. I mean, you must worry about *your* children.
Ray I do — yes — sometimes. You just have to trust them, don't you? I mean, you can only try to bring them up right and —
Rose The thing is, there's no shame nowadays. The more vulgar you are, the more badly you behave, oh it's awful. Anyway, I'm sure yours are lovely, no trouble at all ... now then ... I don't know about you, but I fancy another cup of tea.

Before he can say yea or nay, she's collecting the mugs. She goes into the kitchen

Ray looks at his watch and sighs. Bloody hell

Grace returns

Ray All right?
Grace Still out to the world.
Rose I'm going to make another cup of tea.
Grace Oh — lovely. (*Sotto voce*) You sure it's all right you staying, Ray?
Ray Absolutely.
Grace You've got such a long drive home.
Ray An hour tops.
Grace I can get her a taxi, honestly.
Ray Don't worry about it — as long as *you're* OK me being here.
Grace Of course I am.
Rose You've got no milk.
Grace There's enough there, surely?

Act I   23

Rose For half a cup perhaps. Honestly, Grace.
Grace We'll have to go without then, won't we?
Rose Did you not notice?
Grace For some reason, my mind was elsewhere.
Rose Sarcasm again.
Grace No, I didn't notice.
Rose How can you not have any milk?
Grace I'll get some later — all right?
Rose Did you not get any in?
Grace No — I didn't.
Ray I'll nip out and get some, shall I?
Rose *I'll* go, Raymond. I could do with a little walk anyway. Clear my poor head. (*She's already collecting up her stuff*) Whereabouts is it?
Grace Are you sure?
Rose Oh do stop fussing.
Grace You turn left out of the door and there's a little supermarket down on the right. D'you want some money?
Rose (*ignoring this*) Is there anything else you've forgotten? Bread? Butter?
Grace Just the milk, Mum.
Rose Are you sure? You don't want your husband complaining.
Grace Press the button and I'll let you in.
Rose Fancy not having any milk.

She exits

Grace has moved across with her

Grace This isn't a very nice thing to say, but I just hope she's gone before Albie wakes up.

She's said it lightly enough but clearly means it. Ray gives a little smile, nod. She sits. A moment

Grace I could crown him.
Ray (*grinning*) Yeah.

Another moment

Grace *Did* you think I was a bit of a sad case?
Ray You mean —
Grace Yes.
Ray It was a long time ago, Gracie.

Grace Yes. Silly of me to ask.
Ray No, just —
Grace It was. Silly.

This moment

Ray Not a sad case, no. Just someone on her own.
Grace I did feel very self-conscious. She was right about that, Mum: I wasn't much of a mixer. I'm better now — I've made myself be, but — in those days.
Ray You *went* though, didn't you? On your own. That must've taken quite a bit of doing.
Grace She didn't think I would, you know. But I was determined. I just ... wanted to show her.
Ray Aye, you said.
Grace (*not heavily*) Did I?
Ray You know.

She doesn't know what he means, but nods anyway

Grace Anyway. Whatever the reason, it was for the best, wasn't it?

This moment

   How did you meet Debbie?
Ray I've known her since school.
Grace (*smiling*) Childhood romance.
Ray Not really. We never went out or anything. Not until much later. We'd all gone to see a concert and I asked her if she fancied coming out with me next week and it, you know, started from there.
Grace She's a lovely girl, Ray.
Ray She is.
Grace I hope she knows what a good man she's got.
Ray Sometimes. When I've earned enough Brownie points.

They smile at each other

Grace No. She thinks the world of you. You can tell.

This moment

   Have you ever been back there?
Ray You mean —

Act I

Grace Yes.
Ray No.

This moment

Have you?
Grace I did think about it. But no.
Ray I think it's changed a lot.
Grace Yes.
Ray Same everywhere though.
Grace Seems to be.

A moment

Ray We had a great time there.
Grace Yes. Thanks to you two.
Ray I've got some great pictures. I can show you if you like.
Grace I would.
Ray We'll fix up an evening or something.
Grace Lovely.

This moment

You really did look after me, didn't you?
Ray We just — got on well, didn't we?
Grace That's what I never really understood.
Ray What's that?
Grace Well ... if there had been two of us ... you know — two girls, two chaps.
Ray Two blokes on the pull, you mean.
Grace Well, it happens, doesn't it?
Ray Let's be honest, it usually is when two blokes go off together, unless they're — you know — but ... this time, no, it wasn't like that.
Grace You *did* take pity on me, didn't you?
Ray Gracie —
Grace Oh I don't mind, I don't really. You were so nice to me.
Ray You might ask yourself why, Gracie. No — nothing to do with — taking pity — you really shouldn't say that about yourself. It's — being the sort of girl you were. Are.
Grace And what sort of girl's that then?
Ray The sort of girl who made you *want* to be nice to her. Because she was kind and gentle and — trusting.
Grace That's a lovely thing to say.
Ray Well — there y'go — and it's true.

They are both a little embarrassed

Grace You know what: we never said we'd keep in touch. People usually do, don't they, and nine times out of ten it's just that. Talk. But we never said it. I often wondered why. I mean, *I wanted* to say it, but as neither of you said anything ... and I so hoped you would.
Ray I meant to, but ... things happened back home.
Grace Nothing bad?
Ray Just — you know — family.

She nods, not really understanding

Grace I thought Albie might have wanted to.
Ray (*lying*) I remember him saying ... bloody hell, I didn't take her address or anything.
Grace (*smiling, not believing him*) Oh yes?
Ray Straight up.
Grace You're really protective of your little brother, aren't you?
Ray Not always.
Grace (*still smiling*) Oh you are and it's lovely. Anyway. I'll believe you, thousands wouldn't. (*Has a sudden thought*) You must have been with Debbie.
Ray I was — yes. We'd just started getting serious.
Grace That's why you weren't — you know.
Ray On the pull, aye.
Grace But she didn't mind you going off with Albie.
Ray She wasn't best pleased, I seem to remember. I wasn't too happy about it m'self, but ... Albie can be very persuasive when he wants to be — oh not in a nasty way — just — you know — bags of charm, our Albert. Always has had. Well, *you'll* know that. Anyway. It was the last time we had a holiday together. On our own, I mean. Another twelve month I was a married man with a kiddie.

He frowns. It's clearly not the best of memories. This moment

Grace I wonder why *he* never got married? (*Smiling*) Or perhaps he did.
Ray (*smiling at the thought*) No.
Grace But he's had lots of girlfriends.

Ray doesn't answer

Hasn't he?
Ray Well ... single fellah, not bad looking.

Grace Not *bad*?
Ray All right, reasonably good-looking, good job, few bob in the bank.
Grace A good catch then.
Ray If you wanna be caught.
Grace And he didn't.
Ray You must have asked him.
Grace Must I?
Ray Well you do, don't you?
Grace You do, unless —
Ray Unless what?
Grace Unless you don't want to hear the answer. Or you daren't ask the only question you really want to.
Ray (*smiling*) What question's that?
Grace Why me?

This moment

Ray You can't erase another person's history, Gracie love. And you shouldn't want to because, in a way, it's what brought them to you. He really does love you, you know.
Grace You're a sweet man, Ray. (*She lightly kisses his brow*)
Ray I'm a bloody idiot who's dying for a cuppa tea.
Grace I'll see how much milk there is. (*She's already on her way into the kitchen*)
Ray No, no, you're all right.
Grace (*shaking the carton*) Enough for one cup, anyway.
Ray What about *you*?
Grace I'm fine.
Ray Yeah, all right, go on then.

She makes him a mug of tea during the following

Have you had any thoughts about where you're going to live?
Grace Here.
Ray Oh.
Grace Why d'you say it like that?
Ray I dunno really: I just thought ... I dunno really.
Grace It's a lovely little flat.
Ray Aye, it is.
Grace And it's not as if we'll need more space. I mean, we won't be having any children, so ... I mean, I don't think we'll be here forever ... we'll have to see how things go. You never know, we might be grateful to have it.

Ray I suppose, yeah.
Grace If my transfer doesn't work out and I find myself out of a job or something.
Ray That's not likely, is it?
Grace You never know, do you? Especially nowadays. You think you've got a cast iron contract and then they tell you they've gone bust. Anyway. Albie's well-placed, thank God.

Ray doesn't respond. She looks at him

Ray Aye. He is.
Grace Did you say you took sugar?
Ray No, no thanks. (*He fetches the mug*)
Grace I can offer you some biscuits.
Ray No, no, this is fine.
Grace I should have thought —
Ray It's fine.
Grace I'm going to do a big shop tomorrow.
Ray Honestly, this is fine.
Grace Although I wouldn't put it past you-know-who to come back with her arms full. (*She moves across to look out of the windows*) Nice little terrace. And it faces the sun. I'm pleased about that. I'll need to buy some chairs though. And a little table, maybe. And some plants. (*A moment and, still with her back to him*) I often thought about you, you know.
Ray Me?
Grace Both of you. But, if I'm honest, mainly — you know ... (*She remains looking out of the window, then turns, smiling*) Anyway. You had Debbie to go back to.
Ray Aye.

A moment

Grace Albie said he often thought about *me*. Wondering what I was like, wondering what had happened to me. I expect he told you.

She obviously wants him to say yes

Ray Aye.
Grace He said he saw me as this big beautiful blonde driving around in a Porsche, a white Porsche.
Ray (*grinning*) Aye.
Grace Well I'm big, so one out of five isn't bad.

Act I

Ray There you go again.
Grace I don't know what he sees in me.
Ray What he sees ... is what you are.
Grace That's what I'm afraid of.
Ray You daft button.

They smile at each other

I used to think ... not so much what you'd look like ... more sort of ... what you'd be. You know ... settled down ... husband ... coupla kids.
Grace You thought I'd be married.
Ray Sort of.
Grace (*smiling*) Sort of married.
Ray (*smiling*) Sort of thought.
Grace I could have been.
Ray You could.
Grace There's been men.
Ray I'm sure there have.
Grace Well, boyfriends. No one that I've ... you know. Until all these years later and ... I met Albie again. (*She dwells on it for a moment and then brightens*) You know, when he spoke to me, when I realized who he was, I could hardly say a word. I was right back to where I was, tongue-tied again. God knows what he must have thought. Assistant manager of a grand hotel and not able to string two words together. That was what, six months ago. And here we are, married. Admittedly, me in here with the best man and him in there drunk, but nevertheless, married. (*A moment*) Do you believe in God?

He looks up at her

I know it's a funny question, but do you?
Ray Me?
Grace Do you, though?
Ray Sometimes. I mean, there must be *something*.
Grace That's it, isn't it, that's what I mean ... there has to be a reason ... there always *is* a reason. God, fate, call it what you like, there's always a reason that things happen. I've always believed that, I've always believed there has to be *something*. Like why I never got married. I had offers, but it never seemed right. Sometimes I wanted to say yes just for the sake of getting away, of showing that I *was* worth something, but that would have been wrong, unfair, wouldn't it? And there was always something ... something ... that was telling me no, you've got to wait. You've got to be sure. And then ... when I met

Albie ... I knew that this was why I'd waited, this was the reason. (*She looks at him directly for the first time*) I mean — why else?

A moment and he nods, trying to look understanding

Grace You think I'm wrong.
Ray No.
Grace You see ... that's the one thing I agree with her about — Mum — so many important things in life begin by chance. But *is* it chance?

She clearly wants affirmation of this belief but he can't give any

You think things don't happen like that.
Ray I don't know, Gracie.
Grace But I *do*, you see.
Ray (*sharply*) Then that's all right, isn't it?

His tone takes both of them by surprise

I mean ... what am I supposed to say? You've told me how you feel and that's — that's fine. It doesn't matter what *I* think, what anybody thinks. It's you. Him.

This moment

Grace I'm sorry.
Ray You don't have to keep —
Grace You being a friend ... someone who was there —
Ray What is it you want, Gracie? What is it you want me to say? (*Again his tone jars*)
Grace I want you to understand. I want someone to understand.

It's almost as though she's desperate. A moment and she attempts to lighten the mood

I don't know about you but if it's always like this, I think maybe the best man should get paid.
Ray (*smiling*) I'll put me bill in.

They smile. A moment

Grace Must be all the excitement I suppose. Sorry.
Ray You don't have to apologize, Gracie.

Act I   31

Grace No, I shouldn't have ——
Ray You don't have to apologize. Not for anything.

This moment. Then he suddenly remembers and digs into his breast pocket

  Talking of photographs ... I've got one here that'll make you laugh.
Grace Of us?
Ray I dug it out especially ... that Irish chap took it ... the three of us ... d'you remember him, the Irish chap?
Grace Er ... James, wasn't it?
Ray I think you're right. James ... him and his wife. From Belfast, I think it was. Here. (*He shows her the rather dog-eared photograph*)
Grace Good God.
Ray Told you.
Grace Good God.
Ray I know.
Grace Look at those haircuts.
Ray Horrible.
Grace You look like twins.
Ray We look like a couple of idiots.
Grace I remember exactly when it was taken.
Ray Just after that — waddaya call it — knobbly knees competition.
Grace Knobbly knees competition.
Ray What a memory.
Grace (*pointing*) That's why he's got his trousers turned up.

She returns the photograph to Ray who looks at it, half smiling, half confused

  He came second if you remember.

The downstairs door buzzer sounds. Grace moves towards the door, as Ray continues to look at the photograph

Ray Who did?
Grace Albie, you fool. Look at the silly grin on his face — how could I not love him?
Ray But the thing is, Gracie ... that's not Albie, that's *me*.

She stops in her tracks and turns to look at him. The smiles on their faces have frozen. She slowly moves back, takes the photograph, looks at it, looks at Ray

The bedroom door opens and a bleary Albie appears. He has no jacket, his shirt is unbuttoned and he is holding his shoes

Albie I'm not going to be very popular, am I?

He stands, mock sheepish. The door buzzer sounds again, insistently

CURTAIN

ACT II

The same. A moment or so later

The buzzer still sounds. Albie still stands in the bedroom doorway. Grace and Ray are still looking at each other. She snaps out of it

Grace Excuse me.

Grace rather brusquely shoves the photograph to Ray and goes into the lobby

Albie She's not leaving me already, is she?
Ray She's letting her mother in.
Albie Pity anyone ever let her out.

Grace reappears

Grace She needs a hand up with the shopping.

Her mind, not surprisingly, is still elsewhere. But she realizes

Sorry, darling.

She goes

Albie Don't worry, we've got the rest of our lives. (*He sits, shoes in hands. Realizing*) Shopping?
Ray You've run out of milk.

Albie gives a little jerk of the head. Ray realizes he is still holding the photograph and discreetly pockets it as Albie, with considerable effort, starts pulling on his shoes

Albie (*again realizing*) Why is she still here?
Ray She's getting the next train.

Again Albie gives a little jerk of the head, again makes to put a shoe on

Albie Why are *you* still here?

Ray I'm taking her to the station.
Albie What's wrong with a cab?
Ray You're right. I'll leave you to it. (*He stands*)
Albie Hang on, hang on. Maybe you should — you know. Stick around. I might need a bit of back up. Anyway. If you've said you'll take her.

This moment. Ray sits

   You're a prince.
Ray Yeah, well.

Albie has got his shoe on. He looks blearily ahead

Albie I've got a terrible bloody headache.
Ray You do surprise me.
Albie It's not like me though, is it? I mean, if there's one thing I can do, it's hold me drink.
Ray Trouble is, you were holding everyone else's.
Albie Bloody hell. (*He shakes confetti from the other shoe and has a sudden thought*) You don't think someone was playing silly buggers, do you?
Ray Silly buggers?
Albie With the drink.
Ray (*disparagingly*) No.

Albie clearly isn't so sure but puts his shoe on

Albie Grace is all right, is she?
Ray Fine.
Albie What a start.
Ray She's fine.
Albie Bloody hell. Did she say anything?
Ray (*guiltily*) What about?
Albie Waddaya think — *me*.
Ray No. Albie ——

He almost says something about the photograph, but realizes it would be wrong and anyway Albie is indicating "hold it", up on one hip, pulling his iPhone from his trouser pocket. He focuses on the screen, decides it's a call he doesn't want to take and shoves it back into his pocket

Albie What?
Ray Forget it — nothing important.

Act II   35

Grace and Rose come in. Grace is carrying two supermarket bags. Rose is exaggerating her breathless stair climb

Rose (*seeing Albie*) Oh, hello, Albert. How are you feeling?
Albie Ashamed of myself.
Rose Nonsense.
Albie (*standing, shakily*) Please accept my apologies.
Rose You've nothing to apologize for. It's your wedding day, these things happen. Now do sit down before you fall down.

Albie sits. Grace takes the bags into the kitchen. She and Ray studiously avoid eye contact

I'll do that, lovely — you look after your husband.

She smiles sweetly at Albie and goes into the kitchen. She busies around, humming softly to herself as Grace moves to gently kiss the top of Albie's head

Grace (*fondly*) I could crown you, Mister.

He reaches up, takes her hand, and kisses it

Albie I'm a bloody idiot.
Rose Things are much cheaper up here, you know. I was surprised.
Albie Are you still talking to me?
Grace I haven't decided.
Rose Don't you think, Grace?
Grace Sorry? Oh — yes.
Albie (*to Grace*) Have you got a Nurofen or something?
Rose There are some in my bag, Grace.
Grace I've got some, thanks.

She kisses Albie's head again and goes into the kitchen where she fills a tumbler with water and takes out a packet of pills. Ray watches all this somewhat uncomfortably

Rose It's a lovely flat, Albert.
Grace How many?
Albie Seven. D'you like it?
Rose It's lovely. Very modern. I was saying, wasn't I, Raymond?
Ray Er ...
Rose And just the right size I would have thought.

Albie Whatever the size, there'll always be room for you, Mother-in-law. Right, Mrs Rodway?
Grace Absolutely.
Rose Well, we'll see, shall we? The thing is, Albert, I don't ever want you to think of me as interfering.
Albie I can't see you ever interfering.
Rose You old sprucer.

Albie looks to Ray for explanation

Ray Flatterer.
Rose My son — may I tell you this, Albert?
Albie Please.
Rose My son has been married over twelve years — well, on and off, his first wife showed herself to be, well, not very nice at all — and I'm sure he'd be only too pleased to tell you that I'm the last to interfere but first to offer help should any be required.
Albie (*gravely*) I'll most certainly remember that.

Grace gives Albie two pills and water. He smiles his thanks and takes the pills, swallowing them like they are the size of golf balls during the following

Rose Mind you. Living so far away.
Grace Not so far nowadays, Mum.
Rose Anyway. (*She pats her knees decisively*) You won't want me here, not now, you'll want to be on your own.

Which, apart from anything else, makes Ray feel more than a little awkward and he half-stands

Albie You're all right, no need to rush.

Ray sits down again

Rose I said to Grace, didn't I, lovely, I should go.
Grace So you did, yes.
Rose I said to her, he won't want to wake up and find me still here, of course he won't.
Albie Which is very considerate of you.
Grace Consideration's your middle name, isn't it, Mum?
Albie However ... we've hardly said two words since you got here.
Rose Oh I'm sure there'll be plenty of times for meaningful conversation.

Act II

Albie's phone vibrates again and takes it out, checks the caller and shoves it back into his pocket, throughout the following

Albie I'm sure there will but I'd feel very remiss if you went off before we had the chance of a little chat, don't you think, Gracie?
Grace As Mum says, I'm sure there'll be plenty of —
Albie Seeing as how it's the first time your mum and me have met and I haven't exactly endeared myself to her, I'm sure I haven't.
Rose As I say, these things happen. Oh well ... if you're sure ... I can always catch the next one, can't I?
Albie Or you could always stay.
Grace Stay?
Albie Aye.
Grace Here?
Albie In a hotel.
Rose That's very nice of you, Albert, but I must get back for the cat.

Nevertheless, she makes it clear that she is settling in

Grace Well if you are staying, I don't think we can ask Ray to wait any longer.

Again Ray half-stands

Albie You're all right, aren't you, Ray?
Ray Well, if Gracie would rather ... (*He doesn't know whether to stand or sit*)
Rose As I said, I'm more than happy to get the bus.
Grace We'll get you a *cab*.
Ray Well, if you're sure.
Grace Yes, thank you eversomuch, Ray, you've been really helpful, I've really appreciated it but I really think it's time for you to go home to your wife.
Rose His wife isn't there.
Grace Mum — please.

Ray gives up and sits

Albie Waddaya mean she's not there?
Rose The last thing I want to be is any trouble.
Ray She's babysitting for Sam.
Grace Yes, but you'll still want to get home, I'm sure you will.
Rose (*insisting*) I'll take the bus.

Grace You know perfectly well we wouldn't put you on a bus. Tell her, Albie.
Albie We certainly would not.
Grace You see?
Albie You can use my bike.
Rose (*beaming*) Saucy.
Grace I really think —
Albie You're not in a hurry, are you, Raymond?
Ray Well —
Albie She gives you some stick, you can blame *me*.
Ray (*knowing full well*) If you mean Debbie —
Albie She doesn't like me, his wife. Thinks I'm a bad influence. (*He grins, winks at Rose*)
Ray She knows I'm going to be late and she's quite happy.
Albie There you are then. Besides, like I said, I need you to help convince my new mother-in-law what a wonderful fellah I am.
Grace Well, I don't think it's right.

Albie gives a slow grin and points a finger at Grace and Ray in turn

Albie What's going on?
Grace }
Ray } (*together*) Going on?
Albie Have you two had a row?
Grace (*quickly*) Why would we have a row?
Albie You can hardly look at each other.
Ray Don't be so daft.
Albie I know that look. (*To Rose*) He has this look when he's up to something. (*To Grace and Ray*) Something's going on, I know there is. (*He's more teasing than serious*)
Grace You're just being silly.
Albie (*tapping the side of his nose*) Husbands know these things — don't they, Mrs A?
Rose My husband spent most of his time in the shed.
Albie I can see that I'm going to have to keep my eye on you, Mrs Rodway. And *him*. We know all about the quiet ones, don't we? (*He again taps the side of his nose, and stands*) In the meantime, I'm going to throw some water in my face. Liven myself up a bit. (*He moves to the bedroom door*) Please feel free to continue whatever it is you're up to: I am, after all, only the breadwinner. Well, one of the breadwinners.

He goes into the bedroom

Act II   39

Rose You haven't had an argument, have you?
Grace No, of course we haven't.
Ray Nothing like.
Rose It's not about me, is it? As I've said, time and time again, I'm quite happy to ⎯
Grace We haven't had an argument. Now for goodness' sake.

Rose gives a sulky little shrug

Rose I'm only trying to help.
Grace How? How are you trying to help?
Rose Well ... if you'd had an argument.
Ray We haven't.
Rose No, but if you had.
Grace All right, what would you do?
Rose Well I'd ... mediate.
Grace You don't *know*, do you?

This moment

Rose Is this confetti?
Ray It was in his shoe.
Rose If it was me, I'd clear it up, before it gets trodden in.
Grace I'll do it later.
Rose It gets right into the carpet.
Grace I'll do it when you've all gone.
Rose Where's your vacuum?

Grace knows there is no point in arguing

Grace In the cupboard by the front door.
Rose No, no, I'll fetch it.

Not that either of them looked like doing so. She moves to the alcove

   It's like sand, confetti. Gets everywhere. I used to dread going to Margate but your father insisted. Like he insisted on so many things.

She goes into the alcove

Grace (*sotto voce*) What are you trying to do, Raymond?
Ray (*the same*) Me?
Grace Why are you creating an atmosphere?
Ray Gracie, all I'm trying to do is do what I said I'd do and go home.

Grace I'm not so sure about that.
Ray What d'you mean?
Grace What I mean is, you're trying to make a mountain out of a molehill.
Ray Are we talking about that photograph?
Grace Where is it?

He gives it to her. She looks at it and thrusts it back at him

> Thank you — and yes, you're quite right, I made a silly mistake. but it doesn't mean anything, anything at all and I'd rather that you didn't pretend it did.
> **Ray** Gracie —
> **Grace** And I certainly don't want you to involve my husband.

Rose appears with an elderly vacuum cleaner

Rose I wonder if you'd be so good as to find a plug for me, Raymond.
Ray (*sotto voce*) Oh — yes — right. (*But realizes*) Right. (*He plugs in the vacuum cleaner*)
Rose If I were you I'd think about a new one.
Grace I'll put it on the list.
Ray There y'go.
Rose Thank you so much, Raymond.

Rose switches it on and runs it over the carpet. It's rather noisy

> *Albie, towel in hand, appears in the bedroom door*

He is about to shout about the noise, but sees that the purveyor is Rose. He mimes to Grace that the noise is doing his head in, she mimes that she's sorry but what can she do

> *Albie returns to the bedroom, closing the door as loudly as he can*

Rose, oblivious, carries on cleaning for a moment and then switches off the machine

Rose There we are. Much better. Would you mind, Raymond? (*Meaning, put the cleaner away*)

> *Ray unplugs it and takes it into the alcove*

I was wondering if he wouldn't like a little something to eat. Albert.

Act II   41

Grace I'll ask him.
Rose A little omelette or something.

Ray comes back in

Rose I was saying, Raymond, perhaps Albert would like a little something to eat.
Ray You'll have to ask him.
Rose Oh I think so. He looks to me like a man with a good appetite.

Albie comes out of the bedroom. He had made himself look tidier and will be a lot brighter

Rose I was just saying, Albert, you look like a man with a good appetite.
Albie Appe*tites*. Plural. Food ... sex ... clog dancing.
Grace Mum was wondering if you'd like something to eat.
Rose A little omelette or something — I got some eggs.
Grace We *had* some eggs.
Rose You had *one* egg.
Grace Yes, all right, but it was a large one.
Albie No, you're all right.
Rose You're sure? It's no trouble.
Albie We'll be going out to dinner soon, won't we, sweetheart?
Grace Not *too* soon, I hope.

He takes her face in his hands

Albie Whenever you're ready. And just the two of us.

He kisses her lightly. Rose can't resist being part of the moment

Rose Anywhere nice?
Albie Somewhere very nice ... now then ... who's for a glass of bubbly?
Grace Oh Albie, are you sure?

He's already on his way into the kitchen

Albie Am I sure? Am I sure? On our wedding day?
Grace Yes, but —
Albie I'll have none of that, Mrs Rodway ...

He straightens up from the fridge with a bottle of champagne, puts it on the counter, gets four champagne flutes out of a cupboard and opens and pours the champagne during the following

So then. You've been looking after the ladies, have you, Raymond?
Rose He's been a real treasure
Albie Aye, well he's like that, Raymond. You've still got your boy scouts' uniform, haven't you Raymundo?
Rose How he carried you up those stairs, I've no idea.
Albie Ah well, he was a fireman.
Rose I know, he said. Did you ever save anyone's life, Raymond?
Ray Not by carrying them out of a burning building, if that's what you mean.
Albie But you did get a lot of practice though — give these to the ladies, there's a pal.

He has poured two flutes. Ray collects and gives one each to Rose and Grace

Mind you: not just a fireman. You've turned your hands to quite a few things, haven't you, Ray?
Ray I suppose I have, yes.
Albie (*to Rose*) He even did a spell as a vision enhancement engineer.
Rose Oh yes?
Ray Window cleaner.

He says it automatically: it's the hundredth time Albie has made his "joke"

Rose The man who does mine is Polish. That's what I mean, you see.
Albie Me? Two jobs since I left school, how boring is that? (*He hands a flute to Ray and makes a toast*) To my beautiful wife, my lovely mother-in-law and my big brother on whom I can always depend no matter what — cheers.

They drink, ad-libbing cheers

Rose Lovely.

Albie knocks his back

Albie Which reminds me ... (*He pulls out his iPhone, keys in a number and listens, rocking his head, blah-blah-blahing at the recorded message*) Max? Albert. Those plans you want me to look at. I can do eleven o'clock tomorrow, you choose where. Cheers. (*He ends the call*) Sorry about that.
Rose Your work must come first.

Act II   43

Albie Yeah, it's a big one. (*His mind is already on his text messages so that he is scanning the iPhone*)
Rose You've had a lot of calls, I must say. I didn't speak to them, they're on the answering thingy. I expect you'll want to listen to them.
Albie (*absently*) I will yeah I will, thanks.
Rose You'll have to plug it in first.

He's finished looking at his messages and pockets the iPhone

Albie Sorry?
Rose The telephone.
Albie What about the telephone?
Rose Grace unplugged it.

Grace bites back a retort

Grace (*to Albie*) I unplugged it because I thought it might disturb you and oh look, Mum — I'm plugging it back in again. (*She does, showing each component like a magician*)
Rose I was simply pointing out that Albert might want to listen to his messages.
Albie Pound to a penny they were all women. (*He winks at Grace*)
Rose They did seem to be, yes.
Albie That'll be my harem.
Rose (*smiling wide, but unsure*) Oh yes?
Albie They're planning a mass suicide and they promised to let me know the date.
Rose Someone called Ingrid phoned three times.
Ray (*a shade too quickly*) I said — she's one of the crowd — you know.
Albie Oh — that Ingrid. I thought you meant that married woman I've been having an affair with. Her husband's serving in Afghanistan so it seemed only right to keep an eye on her. I did introduce her to you, didn't I, sweetheart? (*Another wink at Grace*)
Grace Oh — *that* Ingrid. I thought you meant the one with the helicopter.
Rose Now you're just being silly.
Albie I was thinking, Mrs A ... I can't keep calling you Mrs A, can I call you Rose — it is Rose, isn't it?
Rose Yes it is and yes you may. (*The thought really pleases her*)
Albie I was thinking, Rose ... if you hadn't come up, Gracie would have had no one.
Rose D'you know, Albert, I was thinking exactly the same thing. Did you not think of asking any friends, Grace?
Grace I told you, Mum.

Rose She said there was no one she really wanted.
Grace That's right.
Rose Mind you, she's never been much of a one for friendship, have you, lovely? I mean even as a girl.
Grace That's not quite true actually, Mum.
Rose I used to say, bring someone home, let me see who your friends are.
Albie I can't think why you didn't.
Grace (*smiling*) No.
Rose The hours she spent in her room. Reading and dreaming, reading and dreaming.
Grace Not to mention the hours I spent in the bath trying to shrink myself.
Rose Listen to her. How many more times? Long limbs can be very attractive. (*She tries a fond smile on Grace. A moment*) I must say your family seems very nice, Albert.
Albie Oh they are — if someone else is paying.
Rose And how long have you been without your parents?
Albie Oh ... Dad went — what — nine years ago, is it?
Ray Ten.
Albie And Mum — what — four years.
Ray Four years next August.
Rose You must miss them.
Albie We do. We do, yes.
Ray Well ... your mum and dad.
Rose I know Grace misses her father. You do, don't you, lovely?
Grace I do, yes.
Rose She was very much a daddy's girl. I seldom got much of a look in.
Ray That's mostly the way though, intit? Fathers and daughters, mothers and sons.
Albie That's a bit deep for you, isn't it, Raymond?
Rose I do know what you're saying though, Raymond. But there are limits.

Albie has finished off his drink and starts refilling glasses. Rose accepts "graciously". Grace puts a hand over her glass

Ray I'm driving.
Albie So you are. Always does the right thing, this man. Always in control.
Ray Yeah, all right, Albie.
Albie Even when he's out of control, he's in control, you know what I mean?

Rose Apparently Mick Jagger was much the same. Which is probably why he ended up with a knighthood.
Grace The things you know, Mum.
Rose (*to Albie*) As I say, I do a lot of crosswords.
Albie My mother knitted golliwogs.
Rose Yes, well they did in those days, didn't they? (*Changing the subject*) Do you live locally, Raymond?
Ray No — Lytham.
Rose Oh — Lytham. Is that because you like being close to the sea?
Albie No, it's because his wife likes being close to her parents.
Rose I believe the air is very good at Lytham.
Albie And the golf.
Rose Golf I don't know about.
Albie You should take it up, you'd be good at it.
Rose Oh I don't know. All that grunting.
Grace That's tennis.
Rose Whatever. It's not very ladylike.
Albie I love tennis.
Grace I didn't know that.
Albie Oh aye — we used to play a lot, didn't we, Raymundo?
Ray We did.
Albie Most nights in the summer, down the park — never let me win though, did you, you bastard?
Ray No, you've had a tough old life, haven't you?
Rose Do you still play, Albert?
Albie A bit. *We* must play, Gracie.
Rose Oh I don't think so. (*She gives a little laugh*)
Grace Why not?
Rose Well you're not the most co-ordinated girl in the world, are you, lovely? Nothing wrong with that, and no disrespect intended, but it's the truth, isn't it?
Grace I bump into things, yes. Thanks for bringing it up, Mum.
Rose There she goes again.
Albie You bumped into *me* for a start.
Grace I did, didn't I?
Rose Of course, when we called her Grace, we had no idea. Well you don't, do you? As soon as she could walk she was tripping over her feet, weren't you, lovely?
Ray Doesn't everyone?
Grace I don't need defending, thank you, Ray.
Albie Oo-er.
Grace (*half-heartedly to Ray*) Sorry.
Albie (*"confidentially" to Rose*) You see, I'm right —they've had an argument.

Grace
Ray } (*together*) We haven't had an argument.

Grace But you're quite right, Mum: I'm not very co-ordinated. The thing is, it's quite hard when your brain is so far away from your feet

Albie That's how the dinosaur died out.

Rose How she got so stringy I've no idea. I mean, I'm not tall and her father certainly wasn't. Mind you, my son is tall. And they do say it skips a generation, don't they?

Albie That's a bit of a worry.

Rose How's that, Albert?

Albie Well, our father scarcely opened his mouth but our grandfather used to go around at night murdering old ladies — right, Raymondo?

Ray Right, yeah.

Albie suddenly growls and looms over Rose in a Mr Hyde pose. She doesn't notice

Rose We even sent you to dancing classes, didn't we, lovely?

Grace (*flatly*) Yes. Happy days.

Albie The Salford Slayer.

Albie repeats his pose at Rose who again doesn't seem to notice

Rose And singing lessons. We thought it might bring her out. I had quite a nice voice when I was young and I thought she might have inherited it. Oh well. At least she had a good education.

Grace contains herself. Albie, aware of her discomfort, kisses the top of her head

Albie Come and have a look at the view, Rose, you can see the canal.

Rose Oh, I like water.

Albie There you go then — come on, come and have a look at where your daughter's going to be living. (*He takes up his cigarettes*) And I can have a smoke, my wife doesn't like me smoking inside and quite right too. (*He kisses the top of Grace's head. In her ear*) Besides which, it'll give your ears a rest.

She reaches up to squeeze his hand and he briefly kisses her head again then holds out his hand to Rose

(*Very Northern*) Come along, our Rose.

Act II

Rose takes his hand, suddenly feeling like a young girl again, and he leads her out on to the terrace

Excuse us.

Unseen by Rose, he winks at Grace

(*As they go*) You've got lovely soft hands, Rose.
Rose I use a lot of Nivea.

And they are out on the terrace. We will see them throughout the following. There is an awkward silence between Grace and Ray

Ray You really don't have to worry, Gracie.
Grace (*stiffly*) About what?

They will be aware that they can be seen from the terrace

Ray About — me saying anything.
Grace You're not still going on about that silly photograph.
Ray No I mean — you know.
Grace No I don't know.
Ray About — Corfu.
Grace What about Corfu?
Ray Isn't that what you meant?
Grace Meant?
Ray Not saying anything to Albie.
Grace *What*?
Ray About — you and me.
Grace I haven't the faintest idea what you're talking about.

A moment

Ray OK.

He gives a little shrug, smile. This moment. And she can't resist

Grace What are you trying to say, Raymond?
Ray No, you're right, I shouldn't have —
Grace What are you trying to *say*?

This moment

Ray When we looked at that photograph —
Grace Oh stop going on about the bloody photograph.
Ray It brought back memories, that's all.
Grace That's what photographs are for.
Ray I mean of that last day.
Grace I haven't got the faintest idea what you're talking about.
Ray (*gently*) Oh come on, Gracie.
Grace And I do hate being called Gracie. It's Grace. Yes, I know it's very inappropriate, but nevertheless.

This moment

   Well?

This moment

Ray You really don't remember.
Grace (*over-patiently*) Shall I tell you what I do remember, Raymond? I remember meeting two young men, two very nice young men, who, for whatever reason, decided to look after me. I liked them both very much, but one of them I more than liked, much more. That's what I remember and that's what I *want* to remember. (*This moment*) You on the other hand seem to remember things differently.
Ray No, you're right.
Grace You can't just say what you've been saying and then put an end to it with "no, you're right" — I want to know what you're talking about.
Ray I was being stupid, I shouldn't have said anything.
Grace But you *have* said something, haven't you?
Ray I thought you were saying you remembered.
Grace Remembered *what*?

He's obviously having difficulty finding the right words

   Remembered *what*?
Ray That day ... that day we spent together.

Slight moment

Grace What d'you mean — spent together?

Instead of answering, he gives a little shake of the head

   Are you implying —

Act II   49

Ray No ... yes ... I mean, not *implying* ...
Grace I want to know exactly what you're talking about, Raymond. (*Less assertively*) Please.

This moment

Ray I mean ... the day before we — left. Albie had — gone off somewhere — you must remember — and you and I — well, we sat around and had too much to drink.
Grace Ah yes well you can stop right there — I scarcely touched the stuff — I still don't.
Ray Yes, that's true ... but this particular day you seemed to want to talk and maybe you needed Dutch courage.

This moment

Grace And did I "talk"?
Ray You did, yes.
Grace About what?

He clearly doesn't want to answer

About what?

A slight moment

Ray About, oh, everything really. About what you wanted to do ... about your hopes, your dreams ...
Grace (*dismissively*) Oh really ...?
Ray About your family ... about how you didn't want to go back ...
Grace I said all this to *you*.
Ray Yes, Gracie. Grace. To me.
Grace And why would I do that?

He looks at her, then gives a little shake of the head

Why would I do that?
Ray Because you said ... you said you really liked me. And you could talk to me. Needed to talk to me. And because I really liked you. More than liked.
Grace (*stiffly*) You had a fiancée.
Ray A girlfriend. Yes. Which is what made me feel so — guilty.
Grace About *talking* to me?

Ray (*gently*) We went to bed, Gracie. You know we did.

This moment

Grace You're making this up.
Ray No.
Grace Are you saying we —
Ray No.
Grace — because if you are —
Ray I'm not. We wanted to. Both of us. But — we didn't. We just — lay in each other's arms and kissed a little ... and talked. And you cried.

Grace remains looking at him, then moves away and looks out of the window. This moment

Grace Have you said any of this to Albert?
Ray Of course I haven't.
Grace Not that any of it's true. (*She turns*) Is it?

He says nothing

What is it you're getting out of this, Raymond? Are you jealous of him or something? Not because of me, I don't mean because of me — I think you might just be jealous of him because of what he is and what *you* are.
Ray (*softly*) Thanks.
Grace Your mother's favourite, was he? It's often the way with younger brothers, isn't it? I should know if anyone does.
Ray (*softly*) Yes, all right, Gracie, all right.
Grace Feel put out, did you? Love him and hate him at the same time?

She is looking at him almost cruelly. This moment

I didn't mean that. I really didn't mean that. I — I just don't understand why you're doing this.
Ray As I say ... I thought you remembered too.
Grace Tell me this then, Raymond: if it was such a — meeting of the minds — why would I want to forget it?
Ray I don't know, Gracie.
Grace Well you must have *some* idea.
Ray (*quickly*) I think you've wiped it out of your memory.
Grace And why would I do that?
Ray Because —
Grace Because what?

Act II

Ray Because it doesn't fit in with how you want things to be.
Grace Doesn't what?
Ray I think you've altered things in your head — since you met Albie again. You said it yourself ... you remember what you *want* to remember.
Grace (*quietly*) I didn't say that.

He doesn't argue

Ray You talk about fate, things being — what's the word — pre-determined. And I really believe you. That is ... believe you have that need. And, like I say, what happened that day doesn't fit in.

This moment. Which is broken by the return of Rose and Albie

Rose I was telling Albert about the Three Bridges. Do *you* know about the Three Bridges, Raymond?
Ray I don't think I do, no.
Rose They're just up the road from us. These three bridges, one directly over the other — a road over a canal over a railway line. Brunel built them, I looked it up.
Ray Oh. Brunel. Right.
Rose I say built, I mean designed. It was the Irish who built them. But then they seem to build everything, don't they? Railways, houses, roads, you name it. It's quite amazing when you consider what a small country it is. Or "they are", I suppose I should say. Half of them building houses and the other half blowing them up.

Albie moves to Grace and puts his arm around her

Albie Your mother is a fount of information.
Rose I spend a lot of time on my own. Doing a lot of reading. And crosswords, as I say. Now then — who's for a cup of tea — and some cake, I bought a nice little cake.
Grace *I'll* do it — if anyone wants any.
Albie Aye — go on then.
Grace (*stiffly*) Raymond?
Ray Er ...
Albie Go on, have some cake.
Ray Thanks.

Grace goes into the kitchen

Rose Coffee for Albert, I think, lovely.

Albie Actually ... I'd like a cuppa tea — cuppa tea and a nice piece of Rose's cake. (*He smiles at Rose*)
Rose You're not going away then, Albert?
Grace I said.
Albie Honeymoon, you mean? We're having it later, aren't we love?
Grace I said.
Albie Possibly Australia — in the winter.
Rose Oh, lovely.
Albie We'll see.
Rose Do you have connections in Australia then, Albert?
Albie Relatives.
Rose (*impressed*) Oh.
Ray You never said.
Albie I'm saying it now, our Raymond.
Grace Are you sure you don't want a little something to eat, Albie?
Albie I'm having Rose's cake.
Grace I mean more than cake.
Albie No, you're fine, love.

He smiles at Rose who smiles back, feeling very important. Grace gets the cake during:

Rose When you think. All this because of a chance meeting in a hotel.
Albie Ah now — *was* it chance?
Rose Tell me exactly how it happened.
Grace Mum.
Rose No, I want to know Albert's version.
Grace Version? Thanks.
Rose Go on, Albert.

He decides to play up to her, mainly for his own amusement

Albie Well ... I was booking in and I happened to look across and there she was talking to this other bloke.
Rose You didn't recognize her straight away then.
Albie I saw her looking across at me —
Rose This was where?
Albie In the lobby, the main lobby —
Grace Does it matter?
Rose I'm just trying to visualize it.
Albie — and I thought why is that attractive young woman looking at me like that and then I thought, wait a minute, it can't be and I went over and you had this name tab, didn't you love, and I said I don't

Act II

believe it ... but it was, it really was, and wasn't I the lucky one — and I'll tell you something else, Rose: I wasn't meant to be staying there. I usually stay at a little place in Gower Street but they were closed for refurbishment.

Rose Well I never.
Albie Now is that weird or is that weird?
Rose And after all those years.
Albie "Was it chance or was it heavensent?"
Rose How romantic.
Albie We all know what Gracie thinks, don't we, sweetheart?
Grace (*lightly as she can*) That's not fair.
Albie Fair?
Ray *Fair.*
Grace You're laughing at me.
Albie Not laughing, just saying.
Grace You're laughing.
Albie She turned all those men down because she was waiting for me. (*To Ray*) Can you credit it?
Ray I can as it happens.
Rose What men are these?
Albie That's what you said, isn't it, sweetheart?
Grace Actually Albert ... I really think it's personal.
Albie (*grimacing at Ray*) Sorry.
Grace No, but ... that's between you and me. (*She is holding two plates of cake. She gives one to Albie*)
Rose No cake for me, thank you, lovely.
Grace It isn't *for* you. (*She rather brusquely gives the second plate to Ray*)

Albie digs in cheerily but Ray finds it hard to swallow

Albie (*of the cake*) Lovely.
Rose D'you like cake then, Albert?
Albie Anything sweet.
Rose I must remember. Do *you* like cake, Raymond?
Ray Depends, really.
Rose On what?
Ray On what's in it.
Albie You know my favourite?
Rose What's that?
Albie Apple pie, custard and a big dollop of ice cream.
Rose Did you hear that, Grace love?
Grace I did, yes.

Rose The way to a man's heart.
Albie She's already found it — haven't you, sweetheart?
Rose My husband wasn't much of an eater, sad to say.
Grace I think he ate as much as he wanted.
Rose I used to do him these little treats. All to no avail.

Grace brings them their coffee and tea

Albie Our mother, bless her, made custard that never moved. It just used to lie on the plate, defying you. Right, Raymond?
Rose Did she use egg?
Albie I think she used cement. Probably why I ended up in the property business. Although I can't see a connection between our mother's custard and Raymond cleaning windows, I must say.
Ray (*showing his irritation*) I worked for an industrial cleaning company.
Albie So you did.
Ray Cleaning windows was just part of it.
Albie So it was — and it doesn't make you a bad person.
Rose But it is funny how these things work out, isn't it? Like we were saying about you and Grace. And you do believe in that sort of thing, don't you, lovely? Fate. Destiny. Kismet.
Grace Why use one word when three will do — that's the Welsh side of the family.
Rose What was it Shakespeare said?
Albie (*proffering his plate*) Any more cake?

Grace fetches him another slice of cake

Rose "There is a divinity that shapes our ends."
Albie I thought that was the Rabbi.
Rose No, Shakespeare. I looked it up for one of my competitions.
Albie What do *you* think, Raymond?
Ray About what?
Albie Are you not with us?
Ray I'm trying, but you know how slow I am.
Albie "Fate. Destiny. Kismet."
Ray I suppose ... some believe in it and some don't.
Albie Typical Raymond.
Ray Oh?
Albie Sitting on the fence. You love sitting on the fence, don't you, our Raymond?
Ray I prefer it to talking rubbish, aye.
Albie The trouble with sitting on the fence is that you get splinters up your bum.

Act II

Ray The trouble with talking rubbish is you get to believe you know everything.
Grace Do we have to?
Albie We're not arguing, sweetheart, just sibling banter, right Raymond?
Ray Right.
Albie Ever since we were kids ... jab jab, jab jab. Right Raymond?
Ray Right.
Albie This man is not only my brother ... he's my best friend. (*He pats Ray's knee*)
Rose Anyway. I don't think she means that — do you, lovely?
Grace All right, Mum —
Rose She means the way things work out. Don't you, lovely?
Grace I just think ... you shouldn't laugh at what other people believe in.
Albie Not sure I'm with you there, sweetheart. I mean some things, yes ... but *other* things —
Grace Yes, all right, Albie, all right.

It has been a sudden flash of irritation that takes Albie and Ray somewhat by surprise. This moment

I'm sorry.
Albie (*gently*) Come 'ere ...

He kisses her forehead, puts his arms around her, holding her tight. Something that Rose isn't too pleased about and so she cannot resist

Rose (*to Ray, with a false lightness*) She's always been the same, you know: always so very touchy.

Grace makes to reply but Albie puts a finger to her lips

Albie How's the time?
Rose Yes, I mustn't outstay my welcome.
Grace Oh stop it. (*She pulls away from Albie*)
Albie Come on, sweetheart ...
Rose I'm only saying —
Grace You're only *ever* only saying.
Rose (*over-patiently*) I'm only saying —
Grace "I'm only saying" ... that's all I've ever had.
Rose I don't think this is the time or place ...
Grace Oh come on, you *always* think it's the time and place —
Albie Gracie —

Grace No, I've had enough of it, I really have.
Rose I see.
Grace No, you don't see, you don't see *anything* if it doesn't start with *you*.

This moment

Rose You're quite right, Albert, I should be going — and I'm quite happy to catch the bus, thank you.
Grace Oh don't be so fucking *stupid*.

It's the first time the two men have heard her use such language

Rose That's the sort of language you use now, is it?
Grace It's the sort of language you fucking make me use.
Ray I think maybe ——
Albie Nothing to do with you.
Ray (*ignoring this*) I think maybe I should go.
Grace No, I want you to stay, I really want you to stay.
Albie Grace, love.
Grace I do, I really do. Because ... because ... (*She trails off, seemingly close to tears*)
Rose It seems I made a terrible mistake coming here.
Albie I think we should leave it.
Grace It's been the same all my life ... never here when I want you, always here when I don't.
Rose I see.
Albie Grace, love ——
Grace You said you *weren't* coming — why did you change your mind?
Albie Grace ——
Grace Why?
Rose I'm not prepared to ——
Grace *I* know why ... to show me just how much you didn't want to be here.
Rose Don't be so ridiculous.
Albie Come on, sweetheart.
Grace It's true, it's bloody true. And having got here, she behaved like she always behaves, just like I knew she would ... and I dreaded it, I fucking dreaded it ... you weren't ill, you just have to be the centre of attention, like you've always had to ... birthdays, Christmas, holidays, *not* going on holidays ... all my life you've been a nightmare — and don't bring my father into it — you made his life a misery just like you made everyone else's. I used to sob my heart out wondering why

Act II

you are like you are, trying to understand, trying to make some kind of excuse for you ... but not any more ... not any more. You're my *mother* ... you should have ... you should have ... and this is my day ... *my day* ... and you had to try and ruin it — well you're not going to, you're bloody well not going to.

This moment

Rose I can only thank God that your brother never speaks to me like this.
Grace (*quietly, almost a plea*) When did he last speak to you, Mum? Honestly? When?

This moment. Rose turns a brave face on Albie and Ray

Rose If you'll excuse me, I'll just freshen up a little before I go.

She goes into the bedroom, taking up her handbag and already reaching for her handkerchief

This moment

Grace I shouldn't have talked to her like that.
Albie (*gently*) No, I don't think you —
Grace Not in front of you, especially not in front of you.

He embraces her

I've never talked to her like that ... God alone knows I've wanted to, but —
Albie We'll sort it out, I promise.
Grace No — we won't, we won't ... my whole life she —
Albie Hey. Hey.

He continues to comfort her. Ray looks down at the floor, wanting to be anywhere but here. This moment

Grace I'll just go and see how she is.
Albie If you really think you should.

A moment

Then Grace gives a little nod and, without looking at him, kisses his cheek and goes into the bedroom

Albie Bloody hell. (*He sits*) Is this how it is, married life?
Ray It's how family is. *You* know that.
Albie Yeah. Yeah, you're right.

A moment

   I wonder if I should —
Ray Leave 'em be, I reckon.

A moment. Albie nods. He reaches into his pocket, takes out the iPhone, looks at it, frowns, and pockets it. A moment

   I'm gonna stick my nose in here but if you want me to keep out of it, say so now.

A moment

Albie Go on then.
Ray (*aware of the women in the next room*) Tell your girlfriends to go easy on the phone calls.
Albie (*disparagingly*) Not *girl*friends.
Ray Tell 'em to stop it — it's not fair on her.
Albie You think I'm still fooling around —
Ray No, I don't.
Albie Well, I'm not.
Ray I said.
Albie So?
Ray So make it clear that those days are over.
Albie They're just having a laugh.
Ray For her sake, that's what I'm saying.
Albie (*mocking*) "Her" sake?
Ray Your wife.

Albie looks hard at Ray

Albie You sanctimonious prick.
Ray I mean it. For her sake.
Albie My wife, my responsibility. All right?
Ray I've said my piece. So let's forget about it.
Albie You worried about her, are you, Raymundo?
Ray I'm thinking about the pair of you.
Albie I wonder.
Ray Don't be daft.

Act II   59

Albie This what you were whispering about, is it?
Ray No one was ——
Albie Going behind my back, were you? Doing a bit of spadework? Warning her about me and my naughty past? Or chancing your arm maybe?
Ray (*quietly*) Fuck off, Albie.
Albie You've always had a soft spot for her, haven't you?
Ray (*still quietly*) Fuck off.
Albie Haven't you?
Ray I like her — yes — I always have.
Albie Fancied her you mean.

Ray looks at Albie, shakes his head with some disgust

You know what I think? I think you're jealous.
Ray So people keep telling me.
Albie Of Gracie and me — yeah. I don't mean anything heavy, just ... jealous. From the minute we first met her, you were making your little remarks.
Ray I was looking out for her.
Albie (*disparagingly*) "Looking out for —— "
Ray I know what you're like, Albie.
Albie Oh yes and what's that?
Ray Forget it.
Albie *What's that*?
Ray "See that quiet one over there? You watch me pull her".
Albie Look and learn I think I said.
Ray It didn't work though, did it, Alb? She didn't fall for it.
Albie Didn't she?
Ray Did she?

For a moment it looks as though Albie will respond angrily but instead he gives a sarcastic jerk of the head

Albie No. You're right. She was a good girl and I respected her.
Ray What you mean is you looked elsewhere.
Albie You been carrying this around all this time, have you, Raymond?

He looks hard at Ray who says nothing

That's right, Raymond, I looked elsewhere for my holiday romance while you ran around trying to phone your fiancée — sorry, girlfriend — she hadn't quite got you by the short and curlies then, had she? Not until she told you she was three months up the spout — nice little bit of news to pop into your ear the last day of your holiday, wasn't it? I mean, you've got to admire a woman's guile ——

Ray (*softly*) You bastard ...

Albie — course, you came right back and did the decent thing but then you would, wouldn't you, Raymond, Mr Do As You Would Be Done To, Mr Fucking Nice Guy — shall I tell you something? There are times you make me want to vomit — you always have ...

Ray Why did you marry her, Albie?

Albie Go home, Raymond.

Ray Why her, why Gracie?

Albie Go home.

Ray You know what the word is, Albie? Jack the Lad is feeling his age. Jack the Lad has looked around and suddenly he's frightened of ending up on his own. That's what all those phone calls have been about ... it's not Grace they're taking the piss out of, it's you. Jack the Lad, suddenly frightened of ending up on his own and chancing to meet a nice quiet girl who'll wash his clothes and not ask too many questions — that's what the word is, Albie. What do *you* think?

This moment

Albie (*quietly*) I think you should go away and think about what you've just said. And if you really believe it — brother — I don't think you and I will have much more to talk about.

This moment

Grace comes out of the bedroom

Albie (*brightly*) All right, sweetheart?

Grace Kind of. (*She gives a little half-smile*)

Albie Is she er ...?

Grace I hope so. I'm really sorry. Both of you.

Albie Hey. (*He puts his arms around her*)
Albie breaks away when a somewhat chastened Rose comes out of the bedroom, holding her handbag

Albie All right, Rose?

Rose Fine, thank you, Albert. (*She smiles "bravely"*) Well then ... I had a coat somewhere ...

Ray takes up her coat and holds it for her to put on

Act II

Thank you, Raymond.

Grace takes up the hat and gives it to Rose

Grace We'll see you off, shall we?
Rose I don't think that's necessary, thank you, Grace.
Albie You're sure?
Rose Thank you.
Grace You'll give me a ring when you get home.

Rose smiles her agreement, then turns to Ray

Rose If it's still all right with you, Raymond.
Ray Of course it is. (*To Albie and Grace*) I'll, um, I'll be in touch.
Albie Yeah.
Grace (*stiffly*) You must come round for a meal. You and Debbie.

Ray nods

Ray (*awkwardly*) That, um, that other business. You were right. I got it all wrong.
Grace (*stiffly*) Yes you did. Thank you.

A moment, and Ray moves to the door and waits for Rose. It is clear that Rose and Grace want to say something to each other

Albie We'll, er — we'll wait outside, eh?

  Albie goes out, with an indication for Ray to follow

When they are gone, there is a moment and

Grace I do love you, Mum.

Rose looks at her, gives a little smile, then gives her a brief and cold kiss on the cheek. Grace makes to put her arms around her, but she is already pulling away. She makes to go but, with great effort, turns back

Rose I think it's really sad how little we know about our parents. Other than what they show us. Too late now for you to have children so you'll never really know what I mean. I've done my best, Grace, and sometimes I know I haven't done it very well. I can only promise you that there are many times when I don't like me any more than you do. We've all got our — what do they call it nowadays? — baggage — and sometimes it weighs more heavy than we want it to. I doubt that I'll change: but don't think I never look at myself in the mirror. (*She moves to the door*) If you *are* staying here, you might think about changing those curtains.

Rose goes

Grace sits on the sofa. She doesn't know whether to laugh or cry

After a moment, Albie returns

Albie All right?

She nods, smiles

    Ray'll look after her.
Grace I know.

He stands somewhat awkwardly. He notices the presents

Albie (*pleased to break the mood, holding up one of the presents*) D'you want to open these?
Grace (*turning to see him*) Later maybe.
Albie Pound to a penny they're something rude.
Grace Probably. (*She attempts a smile*)

He sits next to her, putting an arm around her

Albie Well then, Mrs Rodway.
Grace Well then.

This moment. Each with their thoughts

Albie (*not heavily*) What was all that with Raymond?
Grace Raymond?
Albie Him getting something wrong.
Grace Oh ... something about that time. You know. Nothing important.

He decides not to probe further so nods and smiles. This moment

Albie He's a good bloke, you know.

Act II   63

Grace I know.
Albie He really does look out for me.
Grace Yes.
Albie We're just different, that's all.
Grace Not that different.

A moment

Albie Maybe not. No, maybe not. (*He breaks the mood by squeezing her and putting his head close*) What time d'you fancy eating?
Grace Can we think about it later?
Albie Course.
Grace Maybe I could do a little something here.
Albie Whatever you fancy. (*He briefly kisses her cheek*)

Again they sit with their own thoughts

   I think I'll have a shower.
Grace Right.

She smiles. Again he kisses her cheek and gets up to go to the bedroom, but moves to stand behind her

Albie I do love you, you know.
Grace I know.

She reaches up and they hold hands

Albie We're gonna be all right.
Grace Of course we are.

They remain holding hands for a moment and then he moves to the bedroom

Albie D'you fancy washing my back?

She smiles. It's obviously one of his lines

Grace Would you like that?
Albie I'd like it a lot.
Grace How much is a lot?
Albie Oh ... six, three and lots of numbers.
Grace Go on then, Mr Smoothie.

This moment

Albie We are, we're gonna be all right.
Grace I know.

   A moment and he goes

Grace remains sitting. Then she gets up and is moving to the bedroom when the telephone rings

   She pauses, but then continues into the bedroom, closing the door

The telephone continues ringing

Curtain

FURNITURE AND PROPERTY

ACT I

On stage: Breakfast bar
Fridge containing champagne
Cupboard containing champagne flutes
Sofa. *On it*: large hat with silk flower on crown
Chair. *On it*: woman's coat, small handbag containing bottle of pills
Empty glass tumbler
Jug of water
Book of crossword puzzles (for **Rose**)
Pen (for **Rose**)
Telephone
Notepad and pen
Vase
Tea things
Mugs
Plates
Cake

Off stage: Small bridal bouquet, three or four gift-wrapped presents (**Grace**)

Personal: **Rose**: handkerchief
Ray: watch, mobile phone, dog-eared photograph
Albie: packet of cigarettes, iPhone, lighter

ACT II

On stage: As before

Off stage: Two supermarket bags containing milk and eggs (**Grace**)
Elderly vacuum cleaner (**Rose**)
Towel (**Albie**)

LIGHTING PLOT

Practical fittings required: nil

One interior, the same throughout

ACT I

To open: General interior lighting

No cues

ACT II

To open: General interior lighting

No cues

EFFECTS PLOT

ACT I

Cue 1	**Rose** is moving to the kitchen *Telephone rings*	(Page 1)
Cue 2	Telephone cuts out **Albie's Voice** *on answerphone as script p.1*	(Page 1)
Cue 3	**Rose**: "... don't you, Mister?" **Woman's Voice** *on answerphone as script p.2*	(Page 1)
Cue 4	**Grace**: "I don't think so." *Telephone rings*	(Page 10)
Cue 5	Telephone cuts out **Albie's Voice** *on answerphone as script p.11*	(Page 11)
Cue 6	**Ray**: "They are." *Telephone rings*	(Page 15)
Cue 7	**Grace**: "He came second if you remember." *Downstairs door buzzer sounds*	(Page 31)
Cue 8	**Albie** stands, mock sheepish *Door buzzer sounds again*	(Page 32)

ACT II

Cue 9	To open ACT II *Door buzzer still sounds*	(Page 33)
Cue 10	**Grace** gets up and moves to the bedroom *Telephone rings*	(Page 64)

www.ingramcontent.com/pod-product-compliance
Ingram Content Group UK Ltd.
Pitfield, Milton Keynes, MK11 3LW, UK
UKHW021846210426
5322IPUK00022B/501